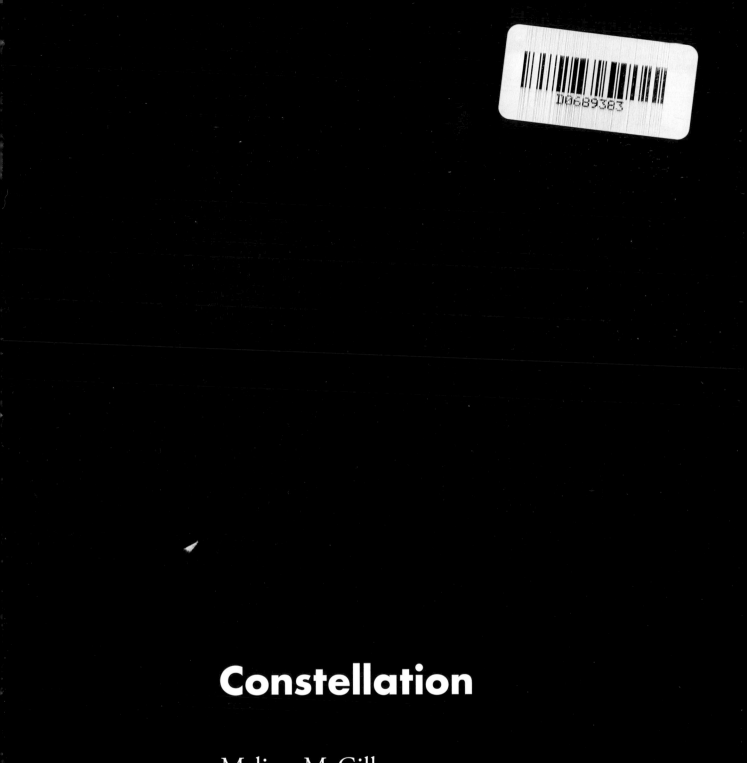

# Constellation

**Melissa McGill**
with Sam Anderson, Joe Baker, Richard Blanco, Hadrien Coumans,
Tracy K. Smith, Edwin Torres, and Jeffrey Yang

Constellation *is dedicated to Mike, Lila, and Henry.*

*Constellation* is a large-scale sculptural installation installed around the ruins of Bannerman Castle on Pollepel Island in the Hudson River.

Every evening, as the sun goes down, starry lights emerge one by one with the stars of the night sky.

Hovering around the perimeter of the castle ruin, these lighted points refer to features of the structure still standing, as well as those details which no longer exist—creating a new constellation connecting past and present through this inspiring light-based public art project—bringing new energy to this majestic part of the Hudson River and the Hudson Highlands State Park.

Reaching further back into the past, *Constellation* references a belief of the Lenape, the Native Americans of the area, of Opi Temakan, the White Road or Milky Way connecting our world with the next.

There are seventeen points in *Constellation*. Each point of light (solar powered LED) is installed on the top of an aluminum pole, ranging in height from forty feet to eighty feet, giving the appearance of each light floating seamlessly in the night sky.

During the day, viewers will see the series of seventeen slender aluminum poles rising from the ruin on the island, creating a visual vertical rhythm around the ruin, drawing the eye upward, while accentuating ideas of absence versus presence.

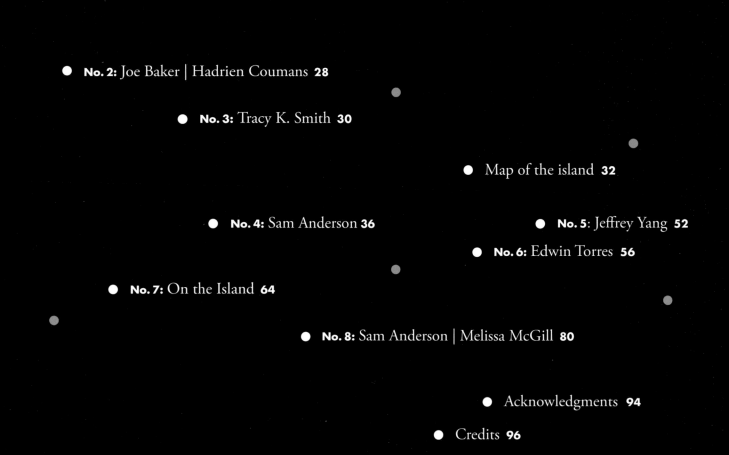

# Contents

# *What are these stars?*

the stars mark a path between

the past and present

light and darkness

heaven and earth

My artwork has always been inspired by pauses, fragments, and negative spaces. And so this island in the Hudson River, with its strange ruin, provoked my curiosity as I traveled on the train along the water's edge between New York City and Beacon. It was not the castle itself but what was missing from it: its ephemeral parallel, the intangible unknowns, the betweens, like the pauses in speech or in birdsong that make real communication possible.

In creating *Constellation*, it was not my interest to solve the island's mysteries or reveal its secrets, but to provide a new connection to this site with its storied and adventurous history and to invoke the long evolution that has led to the ruin we see today.

Rooted in the island and reaching to the night skies, *Constellation* links the past and the present with dreams of future worlds, connects the visible and the unknown, and provides a moment of beauty and reflection during evening excursions.

I have always looked up at the stars for inspiration, for a sense of reality, to remember how small we are in the universe, and to feel how we are all one. I hope *Constellation* brings some of that beauty and wonder to all those who experience it.

—Melissa McGill

**No. 1**

# Richard Blanco

## One Today

*Written for the 57th Presidential Inauguration,*
*January 21, 2013*

Richard Blanco was chosen as the fifth inaugural poet
of the United States in 2013. His poem "One Today" was
written for and read during President Barack Obama's
second inaugural, on January 21, 2013.

## One Today

One sun rose on us today, kindled over our shores,
peeking over the Smokies, greeting the faces
of the Great Lakes, spreading a simple truth
across the Great Plains, then charging across the Rockies.
One light, waking up rooftops, under each one, a story
told by our silent gestures moving behind windows.

My face, your face, millions of faces in morning's mirrors,
each one yawning to life, crescendoing into our day:
pencil-yellow school buses, the rhythm of traffic lights,
fruit stands: apples, limes, and oranges arrayed like rainbows
begging our praise. Silver trucks heavy with oil or paper—
bricks or milk, teeming over highways alongside us,
on our way to clean tables, read ledgers, or save lives—
to teach geometry, or ring-up groceries as my mother did
for twenty years, so I could write this poem for us today.

All of us as vital as the one light we move through,
the same light on blackboards with lessons for the day:
equations to solve, history to question, or atoms imagined,
the *"I have a dream"* we keep dreaming,
or the impossible vocabulary of *sorrow* that won't explain
the empty desks of twenty children marked absent
today, and forever. Many prayers, but one light
breathing color into stained glass windows,
life into the faces of bronze statues, warmth
onto the steps of our museums and park benches
as mothers watch children slide into the day.

One ground. Our ground, rooting us to every stalk
of corn, every head of wheat sown by sweat
and hands, hands gleaning coal or planting windmills
in deserts and hilltops that keep us warm, hands
digging trenches, routing pipes and cables, hands
as worn as my father's cutting sugarcane
so my brother and I could have books and shoes.

The dust of our farms and deserts, cities and plains
mingled by one wind—our breath. Breathe. Hear it
through the day's gorgeous din of honking cabs,
buses launching down avenues, the symphony
of footsteps, guitars, and screeching subways,
the unexpected song bird on your clothes line.

Hear: squeaky playground swings, trains whistling,
or whispers across café tables. Hear: the doors we open
for each other all day, saying: *hello | shalom,*
*buon giorno | howdy | namaste | or buenos días*
in the language my mother taught me—in every language
spoken into one wind carrying our lives
without prejudice, as these words break from my lips.

One sky: since the Appalachians and Sierras claimed
their majesty, and the Mississippi and *Colorado* worked
their way to the sea. Thank the work of our hands:
weaving steel into bridges, finishing one more report
for the boss on time, stitching another wound
or uniform, the first brush stroke on a portrait,
or the last floor on the Freedom Tower
jutting into a sky that yields to our resilience.

One sky, toward which we sometimes lift our eyes
tired from work: some days guessing at the weather
of our lives, some days giving thanks for a love
that loves you back, sometimes praising a mother
who knew how to give, or forgiving a father
who couldn't give what you wanted.

We head home: through the gloss of rain or weight
of snow, or the plum blush of dusk, but always, always
home, always under one sky, our sky. And always
one moon like a silent drum tapping on every rooftop
and every window, of one country—all of us—
facing the stars. *Hope*—a new constellation waiting
for us to map it, waiting for us to name it—together.

**No. 2**

# Joe Baker and Hadrien Coumans
## *Opi Temakan*

Joe Baker is an enrolled member of the Delaware Tribe of Indians and is the Executive Director of the Lenape Center. Hadrien Coumans is the Director of the Lenape Center.

*Opi Temakan*, in Lenape language, translates as the White Road, or the Milky Way, connecting this world to the next. *Constellation* is the *Opi Temakan* in modern expression, bringing light to the historical darkness of indigenous presence by asserting its relation to place. The project is both a natural and constructed installation in which modern consciousness seeks to bridge the seen and unseen. The seen: the island lost to local folk stories, a tourist attraction spanning two centuries, and ruins offering hints of the past. The unseen: centuries of Lenape and Mohican presence extinguished by a genocidal history, defined by great suffering and forced removal.

To many Lenape and Mohican people living today in Wisconsin, Ontario, Oklahoma and beyond, the Hudson River represents their sacred home. The unseen sacredness of place still permeates the landscape despite a bloody history. A people cannot be erased from the face of the earth; the land, waters, trees, boulders, and islands are impregnated by the millennia of living and life. We are still here.

*Constellation* serves as an offering for the future, for all of us today who seek to define our global and interconnected/disconnected world. In its generosity, it bridges the knowing and unknowing and invites questions about the truth of place. *Constellation* prompts the viewer to investigate where we have been, where we stand, and where we are heading. Humbled by the possibility of reincarnation and sensitive to future generations, what we seek today will define where we stand tomorrow.

**No. 3**

# Tracy K. Smith

## from *My God, It's Full of Stars*

Tracy K. Smith is the 2012 Pulitzer Prize winner
for poetry. Her poem "My God, It's Full of Stars"
was originally published in her book, *Life on Mars*
(Minneapolis, MN: Graywolf Press, 2011).

Perhaps the great error is believing we're alone,
That the others have come and gone—a momentary blip—
When all along, space might be choc-full of traffic,
Bursting at the seams with energy we neither feel
Nor see, flush against us, living, dying, deciding,
Setting solid feet down on planets everywhere,
Bowing to the great stars that command, pitching stones
At whatever are their moons. They live wondering
If they are the only ones, knowing only the wish to know,
And the great black distance they—we—flicker in.

Maybe the dead know, their eyes widening at last,
Seeing the high beams of a million galaxies flick on
At twilight. Hearing the engines flare, the horns
Not letting up, the frenzy of being. I want to be
One notch below bedlam, like a radio without a dial.
Wide open, so everything floods in at once.
And sealed tight, so nothing escapes. Not even time,
Which should curl in on itself and loop around like smoke.
So that I might be sitting now beside my father
As he raises a lit match to the bowl of his pipe
For the first time in the winter of 1959.

THE ISLAND

MANHATTAN

## THE ISLAND

**The island is fifty miles north of Manhattan, and one thousand feet off shore.**

**Thom Johnson and Sam Anderson explore what histories are revealed at low tide.**

**No. 4**

# Sam Anderson

## Notes on an Island, Part I

Sam Anderson is a cultural critic at the *New York Times*.

# *What is this island?*

There are too many ways to
answer the question.

*It is a knot of land,*

1000 feet offshore,

that holds, compressed, the entire history of
the Hudson River:

beauty,
revolution,
industry,
decay.

*It is a mystery.*

We don't even know exactly what to call it:
      Pollopel,
Polypus,
                                       Polapis,
                  Pollaples,
                                            Polleppens.


We don't know whether it was named after a cactus
or a lovesick girl or an obsolete piece of sailing equipment.

*We do know that it has a history.*

We know that it was
carved, in an ice age,
by the glacier that
gouged out the Hudson
fjord. The island was
an accident of rock left
in the middle of the
trough.

Then we know nothing for
something like 20,000 years.

# In the centuries since, the island has been used by tribes, patriots, prostitutes, fishermen, bootleggers, vandals.

During the Revolutionary War, American soldiers built an elaborate underwater wall of spikes there, to keep the British from sailing up the river—but the British sailed right through, unharmed.

At the turn of the twentieth century, an eccentric military surplus dealer built a fantastical castle on the island and stuffed it full of armor and cannons and gunpowder. Eventually it exploded and caught fire, leaving the ruin we see today.

*All of this history, and more, is present and absent on the island.*

In the 1600s, Dutch sailors thought of the island as a threshold between good and evil. North was peace, south was danger. The river below the island was deep, narrow, twisted, and bordered by mountains that funneled the wind: the Hudson Highlands. Above the island it was wide, calm, and easy. Dutch sailors said that a goblin lived in the Highlands—the Heer of Dunderberg—who brought storms and ruined ships. During bad storms, living sailors claimed they could hear the voices of the dead—ghost captains calling out useless orders. These legends went on for a long time. First-time sailors of the Hudson River gorge were dipped ceremonially in the water next to the island to inoculate them against the Heer.

In *Moby-Dick* (1851), Melville compares Captain Ahab's insanity to the Hudson Highlands. Occasionally, the narrator tells us, Ahab seems a little less crazy than usual. In these cases, however, his insanity has not gone away—it has only deepened and narrowed, like the Hudson River does in the Highlands. As Ishmael puts it: "Ahab's full lunacy subsided not, but deepeningly contracted; like the unabated Hudson, when that noble Northman flows narrowly, but unfathomably through the Highland gorge."

Today, for most people, the island is scenery from a train. Something in America that looks like it should be in Europe. People crane to look out the window. The castle! They invent histories, almost all of which are obviously false. Train mythology.

"Bannerman Castle makes a two-second appearance in the Michael Bay movie *Transformers: Dark of the Moon* as one of the sites, along with Angkor Wat and the skyscrapers of Hong Kong, of the Pillars that transports (sic) Cybertron to Earth." —WIKIPEDIA

The castle also flashes by, as scenery from a train, in Alfred Hitchcock's *North By Northwest*.

## AN EXTREMELY SHORT HISTORY OF BANNERMAN CASTLE *******

Francis Bannerman V, a Scottish immigrant, supported his family by scavenging cast-off junk (rope, scrap metal) from the Brooklyn Navy Yard.

This was the classic immigrant trick: finding value where a new culture sees none, building a life out of it.

But then Francis Bannerman V went off to fight in the Civil War.

In his absence, his son, little Francis Bannerman VI, was forced to leave school to support the family.

He followed the example of his father, using a grappling hook to fish scraps out of the harbor.

Little Francis turned out to be such an enterprising scavenger that, when his father finally came home, the Bannermans were able to open a shop in New York: a military surplus store.

They harvested the residue of old wars and sold it to eager buyers.

The shop became (according to Thom Johnson and Barbara Gottlock, historians of the Bannerman Castle Trust) "a mecca for collectors."

The store's catalog was at first tiny and handwritten.

Then it grew into a printed pamphlet.

Eventually it exploded into a four hundred–page encyclopedia of the history of weapons and war.

The Bannermans sold, among other items, weapons surrendered by Sitting Bull after the Custer massacre and rubber sandals left over from Admiral Peary's expedition to the North Pole.

In 1898, Francis Bannerman VI made a huge purchase: nearly all of the captured military surplus from the Spanish-American War.

This created a storage crisis.

You couldn't keep a mountain of black powder in the middle of New York City.

So Bannerman bought this small island in the middle of the Hudson River.

He started to fantasize about castles, sketching them on the backs of envelopes and hotel stationery.

He invented a crest that told his family's story: the Scottish flag, a grappling hook, a flaming bomb.

Bannerman designed his castle as an optical illusion: it looked bigger, from the outside, than it actually was.

He built it out of scrap metal, blasted rock, brick, and concrete.

He used old bed frames as rebar, ocean buoys as decorative balls.

There was a working drawbridge.

There were cannons all over the island, some from the Civil War.

Bannerman had a dream that, if he taught people enough about the history of war, war would no longer be necessary.

Theater companies and military men came from everywhere to buy his stock.

The castle's upper floors were used for keeping chickens and playing tennis.

Francis Bannerman VI died in 1918, two weeks after the end of World War I.

The castle's powder house exploded in 1920.

Nearly fifty years later, in 1969, most of the rest of the castle went too: a fire with flames two hundred feet high devoured Bannerman's warehouses, lighting up the Hudson Valley, leaving only the walls we see today.

To go into solitude, a man needs to retire as much from his chamber as from society. I am not solitary whilst I read and write, though nobody is with me. But if a man would be alone, let him look at the stars. The rays that come from those heavenly worlds, will separate between him and what he touches. One might think the atmosphere was made transparent with this design, to give man, in the heavenly bodies, the perpetual presence of the sublime. Seen in the streets of cities, how great they are! If the stars should appear one night in a thousand years, how would men believe and adore; and preserve for many generations the remembrance of the city of God which had been shown! But every night come out these envoys of beauty, and light the universe with their admonishing smile.

The stars awaken a certain reverence, because though always present, they are inaccessible; but all natural objects make a kindred impression, when the mind is open to their influence.

—Ralph Waldo Emerson

.

Emerson, Ralph Waldo. *Nature*.
Boston: James Munroe and Company, 1836.

Why would a star ever smile?

In what way would stars, in the aggregate, "smile"?

What would they be admonishing us for or toward?

The stars must have been much more impressive from the streets of the cities of the nineteenth century than they are from the streets of the cities today.

Light pollution. Skyglow. From Fifth Avenue you can see fifteen stars. Baby sea turtles move toward shopping mall parking lots, thinking the stars are there.

Can the same be said of women?

Or would they have different feelings about these hypothetical rare stars?

Do women and men have different thresholds of belief and adoration? Different instincts of preservation? Different attitudes toward future generations?

Why would the stars suggest a city of God?

Why would a city of God not be constantly visible?

In what way are stars beautiful?

What if we could get to them?

**No. 5**

# Jeffrey Yang
## *Line and Light*

Jeffrey Yang is a poet and editor of *New Directions*.

**I.**

Ceiling turned to sky

Time to timelessness

Further from the center to the outer stations, along darkening tracks along opposing banks

Through the fjord the sound, river iced over

Night valley emptiness, seawater tide, shored

Against wreckage, for a new form to live by

Runs the line, out, on and ahead, reaching toward, into

Now held by the light of the end, here

Of what was and to come, past the storm-cloud mountain

City of broken glass, circle of boulders, lightning-rod field

Scholar-rock memory, floating gate in the middle sea: eagle-shadow, tower break-

Water, frozen fragments, cracking sheet, silence of life beneath

Wind swirls the snowgrains, echoes raised in the breath, the pause

Fading moon at the last-quarter, wild grass not dead but asleep

Steady iamb of freight cars from the other side, breaking free

Island apart, between, negative halo hovering

Moment, of the radiant spheres, burning asterisks

## II.

Darkness goes to dawn as the lights fade and the lines appear, formless shadows beginning to shape the nature of surroundings.

Poles set horizontally across the meridian would make it appear to be a construction site, or a cage, from a distance, recognizable screen.

But with space between the lines the evidence of what was extant merges into the clouds of the mind as different signals or signs.

Morning's ordinary stillness: listening for the horses-of-the-Frisians lapping the waves, hearing the crosstalk of autumn birds.

The flute of the orchards brightening blue, the way whitecaps play against a barge drifting slowly toward the remembered city.

Time reverses in the golden light, the reds and yellows blur the frame into a postcard signed "Love, M. M."

Everything was made to matter—out of spirit.

Seventeen echoing a hidden significance when measured against the proportions of the collapsing structure.

Even now, following this track of influence and arriving on the little island, overgrown, wild with green plants and trees, plastic chairs, rubble, beer cans, new metal reinforcements against a history of natural destruction.

Above the grottoes and cisterns the vertical screams.

Set in a former room by the former stairs spiraling topography into air.

How sight follows the real, hollow becomes hub, cave an inner exaltation.

*Noble deer,* swimming toward the island in the summer rain, when lightning was a god's fury, hidden gods, of forest and current, *tawhid* oneness in unity, what hoped for fidelity, in the absence, along the bone-scattered shore, hart's ribcage, red-winged trill.

Vines cling to the mortar binding the crumbling brick wall.

River-moat provided safety and protection to the castle arsenal, built with cement and junk sealing brick, cannonball ornaments, rope-patterned juttings, faggot burner atop corbelled cylinders, capstan and sally ports, ramparts to pilasters, finial buoys on buttresses, steps to wee bay, Gatling guns on sun-porches, now portcullis emptiness, powdered memory of a flint economy hosting new wars.

Picturing facts: exposed juniper berries, voices of hikers descending, water celery swaying in the shallows, inert stones, the painted lines blending into translucent spheres, gesturing before that, before that…

Their points of interrelation cannot manifest themselves but in the artifact that swells and glows.

**III.**

Last light dims to first light

Standing on a platform looking through the dusk

At the holi fire-yellow dusting the brae branches like corn pollen

Sprinkled in curving rows and spirals of a hidden truth

The passing names, imagined lines, what exists as a renewed sense of place

Night, day, night rhythm of architectonic projection

Darkness slowly deepening with filaments igniting, one by one

Translating the sun, each luminous body filling the space within it

One pause, then another, listening to a *beehive of light* switch on

Seeing the island as if from the other side of a celestial mirror

As if these same words were already written but with different meanings

On a slope shadow of a cypress rising out of nothingness into the open

Against the distant lights of the houses, each point at rest locates its fullest intensity

Unaware at the time this was an emblem of happiness

Moths circling the glass, nature dissolves the mind

How conquest becomes decay, disrupting the perimeter

Of the constellation: line and light, figure and void

Edwin Torres is a poet and artist.

## POLLEPEL ISLAND

what is that part of me floating in the water that i cant touch
that collection of mystery interwoven by dust and daze
how far am i trying to extend this reach so i can swipe a part of my past
just out there, surrounded by water, another island to claim
another intersection in the byways

in a field of water, an island will surface
as often as it is gazed upon
the tips of understructure, invisible
to the looking glass, the fractured nobility
of land in the mess of its grounding

what is the open sine wave from my seat, here on the train
to the empty rooms and hallways of broken brick
out there, on a patch of earth formed by spirits to endear
the imagination, to re-involve the revolvement
of intricate wordplay, at the core of my personal castle

in the dungeons of a supernova, where impulse is a tributary
for reason, a body will rise out of its echo
invisible to the solar reflection, the sheet of glass
masquerading as sky, in the mess of celestial
blind spots

who can count on fingers, align the proper number
of lines in a poem for permutations of obscurity
to latch onto incoherent talismans, out there
the interplay of satisfaction with reversal,
a dome to submerge most imperfected hearts

in the borrowed inversion of another poem, is where
the brother remembers the blood, the coursed
enveloping that frames a sunrise
out of its reflection into the woven path, the daisy chain
of neuro seers, that cleans up the mess

## STARGAZER: CAN THIS BE ABOUT WALKING OR DOES IT HAVE TO BE ABOUT FINDING

emblems appear to the unexpected
who wait for nothing — who travel *inside* waiting
the beyonding step of our externalized…

>                    …*stay here with me*
>                    *outside these waters*
>                                   *my isolation*
>                    *a step from yours — my other*
>                                   *as I point, yours*

there you passed me again — stepping through
the largest drop, the highest cloud
the stretch between the impossibles…

>                    …*how to find the reason*
>              *to leave what you are*
>                         *for a glimpse*
>                    *at the thought you were*

internalize the step — for the reach
to go, externalize the reach
and the distant mission…is not so far anymore

. . . .

there, again — astounding
how silver and skinny moonman can get, didn't anyone
tell him to mind his body image — a wreck of a mirror
there, the shade behind the object
becomes the object…

>              …*shadow be stain*
>         *on sunlit night*
>              *point my connectors*
>                    *and move — who said*
>              *load — was heavier than — soil, soul, sol*

emblem of scar-lit night
ripped across orange slit
through sunset
blood of wind
through north-less light
sun might you go
where nowhere knows
what is your body image
how do you see yourself
alone at night
on the other side
away from the curved
horizon that runs my line
the curved rim
that leads my sleep

. . . .

swallow the ranging tendril, the covered inhibitor
the outter interruption — at the service of range
deserving its loaded tendrils…

       *…come to me*
    *in a white line*
       *a direction — a needle*
   *moving through ancient i*

obstruction of will — giant night walk
to seek and not find, sacred mysteries at home in ruin
what is the move against hiding that changes finding…

      *…and now, if i walk without pain*
    *will that open the door*
       *take the try i formed, as a lit reminder—*
    *and give it legs*

## CELESTIAL SPINE

the offer of walking
the action on the outside
the sensory invisible

our breathing
our leaving
our machinery of leaving

our expansive thievery
equal to leaving things
where they were

before arriving
before the rivering escape
of we

becomes the encounter
with a practical split
among recognized forms

the cognitve invisible
emboldened
by the walking of the visible

the inside visible
in the swing of our heel
naturally alive

our way to remain
where we are
detached

as our tail remains
re-ttached
before we arrive

## WAYS TO PAINT:
## NUMBERS ONE THROUGH MANY

little castle in the sky
find a spirit in my eye
if i wake before i fly
find a ruler in my eye

little spirit in the sky
find a castle in my eye
if i rule before i wake
find another i to make

little spirit in the sky
find a castle in my eye
if i rule before i fly
find another rule in i

little castle in my i
find a spirit in the i
if it fly before i wake
find a star for me to take

## OBLIQUE OFFERING

and I became the words I started with
the *left alone*
that never made it to my mouth my eyes
my height in conversation
with my fall my one by one
still standing where
I once was

and these were the feet I found
along the broken path uncolored
by lightless night
along the white I ruined and this
was the step that called me
the one I started the *left alone*
that *not* became

and who was the mouth I opened
the mortal impregnation
masquerading as soul not spirit
left free by body of wake of call
of sound that left me
between *this* and *that*
the world of *we* behind the one
we don't

and why did I find what *not* did
when I needed *not*
what formless occupation I invent
when I have *no* words just out of reach
just there, where *no* replaces *not*

for denial for meaning for sound
for oblique assemblages
of higher forces that I will never see
but be

and I became the questions I asked
the incomplete arrangement
of my beauty when I started speaking
and couldn't hear my *not* speaking
my offering of *not*
a measure to leave behind
to offer my children what I was missing
and how beautifully incomplete I was

and I was to find my moves
behind me
forced to find their shadows
by the moves I took to get there
making the breath of the *get there*
be the make that I leave, in the act
of becoming the act

# No. 7

# On the Island

There are seventeen points of light in *Constellation*, that slowly light one by one as the sun sets and hover above the island for two hours before disappearing into the night. Each light is a solar powered LED encased in a hand-blown sapphire blue globe installed on top of a slender aluminum pole. The shades of blue glass vary in intensity. The poles, visible by day, are painted on the bottom to blend in with the architecture and trees then fade gradually to silver as they rise beyond the ruin and appear to float seamlessly in the night sky. At heights ranging from 40 to 80 feet tall, the poles create a visual vertical rhythm, drawing the eye upward while accentuating ideas of absence versus presence and revitalizing the site.

**No. 8**

# Sam Anderson

## Notes on an Island, Part II

# Melissa McGill

## *Reverse Constellation*

## *Punctuation*

This series of two-sided works is a collaboration
with writer Sam Anderson. He chose quotes
or wrote original typewritten pieces responding
to *Constellation*. Melissa McGill used graphite,
pastel, watercolor, Sumi Ink, and charcoal on the
typewritten pages. She then took a Japanese
hole punch and punched out the periods, punctuation, pauses and/or spaces in the written
works to create new constellations, illuminated
when light shines through the page.

Presence is an absence of absence.

Ralph Waldo Emerson, 'Nature'

What to call it.
How to spell it?

Menahtiso
Pallopels
Palopel
Folaples
Polipals
Polipel
Polipels
Pollap
Pollapels
Pollaples
Pollepel
Pollepel's
Polleple
Pollipils
Polliples
Pollopell
Pollopels
Pollopens
Polly Pell's
Polopel
Folopels
Polopens
Polopons
Polypus
Pot Ladle
Potladle
Bannerman
Bannerman's
Bannermans
Cheese

        "an individual star is as
         unusual a thing in our
         universe as an individual
         tree"

When a squirrel moved into a hole in my house, I trapped it and let it go on the other

side of the Hudson River. I trusted the river as a boundary; a ribbon of non-connection.

Then I read in a book about the river that squirrels, in desperate conditions, have been
         "new stars are typically
          formed in associations
known to swim across the Hudson. Benedict Arnold, of course, crossed the Hudson to escape
          with dozens to hundreds
the Revolutionaries he had betrayed. Many squirrels moved into the hole in my house. A
          of stars all forming
          from the same dense cold
river region of the interstellar
          medium.
          But when a massive star
          forms, it spews out so
          much energy that it heats
          up the whole cloud in
          which it formed, bringing
          the process of star
          formation to a halt."


        "The way in which a star
         participates in the
         system of a galaxy
         depends more on its mass
         than anything else."


                              "The time it takes a star to form
                               might, indeed, be called a day in
                               a galactic life."

                                        "one must think of
                                         10,000 years
                                         as if they were
                                         a second"

Lee Smolin, "The Life of the Cosmos"

Artist rendering juxtaposing historical and recent photographs, with stars marking a path between past and present.

**Melissa McGill views *Constellation* from a boat on the Hudson River.**

# Acknowledgments

**Constellation** *is made possible thanks to the efforts of an exceptionally talented team of experts and generous supporters.*

## CONSTELLATION TEAM:

Michelle Alumkal, Sam Anderson, Jeffrey Anzevino, Michael Arginsky, Joe Baker, Lee Balter, Susan Sayre Batton, Jennifer Barry, Bill Bauman, Beacon Arts, Melissa Beck, Richard Blanco, Diane Boujikian, Kit Burke-Smith, Andrew T. Chmar, Elyse Connolly, Linda Cooper, Hadrien Coumans, Brian PJ Cronin, Allison Cross, Michael Devonshire, Deborah Dichter, Kelly Ellenwood, Robert Featherstone, Randall Fleisher, Jonathan Frank, Joseph Fratesi, Ricardo Fuentes, Paul Gallay, Becky Gordon, Beth Haber, Tommy Harron, Donna Hayes, Deke Hazirjian, Kurt Hirschberg, Sommer Hixson, Tom Hole, John Huba, Bob Jennings, Thom Johnson, Jimmy Jolly, Gary Kline, Aryn Kresol, Jo Laird, Christopher Lindner, Jennifer Lippert, John Lipscomb, Mike List, Glenn and Susan Lowry, Alina Lundry, Eve MacSweeney, Jason Makowski, Representative Sean Patrick Maloney, George Mansfield, MJ Martin, Chris McGrath, Andrea Moreau, Patrick Motter, Erin O'Neill, Daniel Oates-Kuhn, Anne and Frederick Osborn III, Taylor Palmer, Anne Pasternak, Libby Pataki, Rob Penner, Dick Polich, Lee Ann Pomplas, Warrie Price, Jeremy Pyles, DJ Rekha, Robert Riccardelli, Garrett Ricciardi, Dan Rigney, Michael Roets, David Ross, Marc Schreibman, Darnell Scott, Kris Seiz, Alberto Sid, Tracy K. Smith, Paris Starn, Bea Stern, Lisa Stern, John P. Stern, Maureen Sullivan, Ned Sullivan, Lindsey Taylor, Maja Thomas, Edwin Torres, George Trakas, Peter Triolo, Thomas P. Tyler, William van Roden, Mary Kay Vrba, Mary Welch, Thomas Wright, Jeffrey Yang, Chris Zezza, Curtis Zunigha

Ace Flag Company, The Bannerman Castle Trust, Beacon Fine Art Printing, Cuddy & Feder LLP, Drake Loeb PLLC, Dutchess Tourism Inc., Fabhaus, Highline Stages, Hudson Highlands Land Trust, Jan Hird Pokorny Associates, The Lenape Center, MAF Technologies Corp/Electronic Design and System Architecture, Manitoga/The Russel Wright Design Center, Metro-North's Partnership and Marketing Support, The New York State Office of Parks Recreation Historic Preservation, Niche Modern, Polich Tallix Fine Art Foundry, Putnam Tourism, Red Art Projects, Red Letter Day Event Planning, Riverkeeper, RSM Custom Painting, Scenic Hudson, Storm King Adventure Tours, Times Square Lighting

## GRANT AND MAJOR SUPPORT:

Anonymous, Available Light of New York, Christopher Buck, Allison Cross, Elizabeth Edelson, The Education Foundation of America, Ella's Bellas, John and Lyn Fischbach, The Freedman Family F███, Ric███ Herbert, Kevin and Marina Krim, Ric███ and Natasha Krupp, LNJ Tech Services, The Lulu & Leo Fund, Brad and Heather McGill, Melissa Meyers and Wilbur Foster, The National Endowment for the Arts, Kathleen O'Grady/The O'Grady Foundation, Anne & Fred Osborn III/The Easter Foundation, Anne Pasternak, The Peter and Carmen Lucia Buck Foundation, Dick Polich/Polich Tallix, Inc., The Ralph E. Ogden Foundation, David and Jeannette Redden, Kris Seiz, James Spindler, Lucy Waletzky

**FRACTURED ATLAS** · **ART WORKS.** · National Endowment for the Arts arts.gov · **NEW YORK** STATE OF OPPORTUNITY. | **Parks, Recreation and Historic Preservation**

## THE ARTIST WOULD LIKE TO THANK:

Mike, Lila, and Henry Quinn
Enid Kessler and Stuart Paris, Brad and Heather McGill, James McGill Jr., Janet McGill
Jodi Levine, Helen Quinn, Jonsara Ruth, Meredith Heuer, and Ivy Meeropol for their extraordinary support

## DRAWING CREDITS:

Pages █–16: *Constellation*, John Huba

Page 81: *Reverse Punctuation Constellation: Gravity Determines Everything*, 2014. Graphite, pastel, charcoal, typewriter ink, punched holes. 8¼ inches wide x 11½ inches high.

Pages 82–83: *Reverse Punctuation Constellation: Presence Is An Absence of Absence*, 2014. Sumi Ink, watercolor, typewriter ink, punched holes. Front and back shown. 8¼ inches wide x 11½ inches high.

Page 84: *Reverse Punctuation Constellation: It*

Page 85: *Reverse Punctuation Constellation: Ralph Waldo Emerson/Nature*, 2014. Graphite, typewriter ink, punched holes. 8¼ inches wide x 11½ inches high.

Pages 86–87: *Reverse Punctuation Constellation: What to Call It*, 2014. Graphite, typewriter ink, punched holes. Front and back shown. 8¼ inches wide x 11½ inches high.

Pages 88–89: *Reverse Punctuation Constellation: Squirrel*, 2014. Sumi Ink, typewriter ink, punched holes. Front and back shown. 8¼ inches wide x 11½ inches high.

**PUBLISHED BY**
Princeton Architectural Press
37 East Seventh Street
New York, New York 10003
Visit our website at www.papress.com

© 2015 Princeton Architectural Press
All rights reserved
Printed and bound in Canada by Friesens
18 17 16 15   4 3 2 1   First edition

ISBN: 978-1-61689-430-6

Every reasonable attempt has been made to identify owners of copyright. Errors or omissions will be corrected in subsequent editions.

Editor: Jennifer Lippert
Design: William van Roden

Special thanks to: Nicola Bednarek Brower, Janet Behning, Erin Cain, Tom Cho, Barbara Darko, Benjamin English, Jan Cigliano Hartman, Jan Haux, Lia Hunt, Mia Johnson, Valerie Kamen, Simone Kaplan-Senchak, Stephanie Leke, Diane Levinson, Sara McKay, Jaime Nelson, Rob Shaeffer, Kaymar Thomas, Paul Wagner, Joseph Weston, and Janet Wong of Princeton Architectural Press
—Kevin C. Lippert, publisher

Library of Congress Cataloging-in-Publication Data available upon request.

**PHOTOGRAPHS BY**
Todd Heisler/*New York Times*/Redux: pages 8–9, 14–15, 92–93
Meredith Heuer: pages 6–7, 10–11, 66–69
John Huba: cover, pages 12–13, 16, 76–79
Rob Penner: pages 2–5, 70–73
Ellis Michael Quinn: pages 65, 74–75